W9-AUI-606

INSIDE THE WORLD OF SPORTS

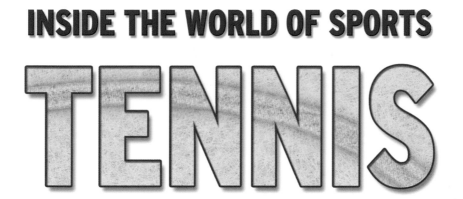

TENNIS

INSIDE THE WORLD OF SPORTS

AUTO RACING

BASEBALL

BASKETBALL

EXTREME SPORTS

FOOTBALL

GOLF

GYMNASTICS

ICE HOCKEY

LACROSSE

SOCCER

TENNIS

TRACK & FIELD

WRESTLING

INSIDE THE WORLD OF SPORTS

TENNIS

by Andrew Luke

MC MASON CREST

Mason Crest
450 Parkway Drive, Suite D
Broomall, Pennsylvania 19008
(866) MCP-BOOK (toll free)

First printing
9 8 7 6 5 4 3 2 1

Names: Luke, Andrew.
Title: Tennis / Andrew Luke.
Description: Broomall, Pennsylvania : Mason Crest, [2017] | Series: Inside
  the World of Sports | Includes webography and index.
Identifiers: LCCN 2016026174 (print) | LCCN 2016026437 (ebook) | ISBN
  9781422234662 (Hardback) | ISBN 9781422234556 (Series) | ISBN
  9781422284285 (eBook)
Subjects: LCSH: Tennis--Juvenile literature.
Classification: LCC GV996.5 .L87 2017 (print) | LCC GV996.5 (ebook) | DDC
  796.342--dc23
LC record available at https://lccn.loc.gov/2016026174

QR CODES AND LINKS TO THIRD-PARTY CONTENT

CONTENTS

KEY ICONS TO LOOK FOR:

Words to understand: These words with their easy-to-understand definitions will increase the reader's understanding of the text while building vocabulary skills.

Educational Videos: Readers can view videos by scanning our QR codes, providing them with additional educational content to supplement the text. Examples include news coverage, moments in history, speeches, iconic sports moments and much more!

Text-dependent questions: These questions send the reader back to the text for more careful attention to the evidence presented there.

Research projects: Readers are pointed toward areas of further inquiry connected to each chapter. Suggestions are provided for projects that encourage deeper research and analysis.

From the clay courts of Paris to the hard courts of Australia, tennis is one of the world's most international sports. Uniquely in the sporting world, the women's professional game developed in parallel with the men's, and both versions are equally popular with fans today.

CHAPTER

TENNIS'S GREATEST MOMENTS

Americans used to be good at tennis. Many of the sport's greatest players are, in fact, from America. From household names like Connors and McEnroe to Courier, Sampras, and Agassi, American men have a powerful legacy in the Open Era. On the women's side, Evert gave way to Davenport, Capriati, and of course, the Williams sisters.

Well into their 30s, Venus and Serena Williams remain the lone Americans at the top of the sport, and it has been that way since Davenport was number one in the world a decade ago. Besides the sisters, no other American man or woman has won a Grand Slam singles event since 2003, when Andy Roddick won the U.S. Open.

The sisters cannot play forever, and the mantle on the men's side has long waited to be picked up. Where is the next crop of American stars? One of the prevailing theories is that there may never be any, and the blame for this may lie squarely on the rackets in the players' hands.

Technology killed the American tennis star. In America, coaches teach the attacking, serve and volley game of Sampras and McEnroe. Players are taught to keep points short, coming in behind powerful forehands. The change from natural and nylon to polyester-based string at the turn of the century has all but eliminated this style of play. The polyester strings produce no spring, allowing players with lightweight graphite rackets to crush the ball with massive topspin from anywhere on the court.

The result is that baseline players have been able to achieve great success by playing offense from the baseline and beyond. Fitness and court position have replaced shot making to a large degree, a change that has benefited European and South American players who grew up on slower courts.

American tennis has been slow to adapt. Tournaments in New York, Los Angeles and San Jose have been relocated to other countries. It may take a few years for coaching to catch up to the way the game is played today, as the next generation of young Americans grows up with the new racket strings and the strategy toward the game that accompanies them.

Meanwhile, the past and current generations of stars, using everything from wood and catgut to graphite and nylon have produced the moments that fans love to watch, no matter what country they hail from.

The Match of the Century

In 1926, Suzanne Lenglen of France was the biggest star in women's tennis. Helen Wills, the demure Californian, was an up-and-coming player who at 20 already had won two U.S. Open Championships and two gold medals at the 1924 Olympics. Wills flew all the way to the south of France for the possibility of facing Lenglen in a tournament in Cannes. Media hype for the "Match of the Century" reached a fever pitch when both women made the final.

Lenglen, with her six Wimbledon titles and flamboyant lifestyle, was regular tabloid fodder. The experience was new for Wills, who would go on to win 19 major titles but did not play her best in this spotlight against Lenglen. Royalty from Russia, Sweden, and India attended the match played in front of a stadium packed with 6,000 fans. Lenglen won 6-3, 8-6 in the only match between the two tennis legends.

1980 Wimbledon Men's Final

From July of 1979 to September of 1982, either Sweden's Björn Borg or American John McEnroe were ranked number one in the world. Borg held the top spot and the number one seed when the two met in the 1980 Wimbledon final. McEnroe, who had a well-earned reputation for being hot tempered and combative with officials, came into the match as the villain in the eyes of the fans. He had been particularly contentious in his semifinal win, so the crowd was backing defending champion Borg, fresh off his victory at the French Open.

McEnroe was undaunted and easily won the first set 6-1. Borg rallied to win the next two, however, and the fourth went to a tiebreaker that stands as a classic. McEnroe prevailed 18-16 in the tiebreaker to force a fifth set, which went without a service break until the 14th game, claimed by Borg for his fifth straight Wimbledon title.

1984 French Open Men's Final

Between that 1980 Wimbledon final and the 1984 French Open tournament, Borg had retired, and McEnroe had won six majors. He was ranked number one in the world, but Czech player Ivan Lendl was a close number two. The two top seeds met in the final, with Lendl looking for his first major and McEnroe looking for his first French Open title.

McEnroe was the heavy favorite and easily won the first two sets, but Lendl rallied to win the third. With McEnroe up a break at 4-3 in the fourth, the match turned when Lendl found another gear and got a service break of his own. He broke McEnroe again in the fourth to win 7-5 and once in the fifth to win that set 7-5. It was the first of only three losses for McEnroe in that remarkable 1984 season. He would never again make it to the French Open final.

Golden Slam

Achieving the Grand Slam requires a player to win all four major tournaments in the same calendar year. Before 1988, only one man, Rod Laver in 1969, and one woman, Margaret Court in 1970, had ever achieved it. In 1988, Germany's Steffi Graf not only completed the Grand Slam but also took it one step further.

Graf started by winning both the Australian and French Open finals in straight sets. At Wimbledon she earned her first title there by winning 12 of the last 13 games in the final. She completed the Grand Slam by dominating the third set in a win over Gabriella Sabatini at the U.S. Open. Just a few weeks later at the Seoul Olympics, she won the gold medal with a straight sets win over Sabatini. No other man or woman has ever won all five tournaments in the same year, a feat dubbed the Golden Slam.

The Fourth Time Is the Charm

In 2001, three-time Wimbledon runner-up, 30-year-old Croatian Goran Ivanišević, had seen his once lofty ranking tumble from second to out of the top 100. He did, however, receive a wild card entry to the 2001 Wimbledon tournament. And what a wild card he was.

Ivanišević made an improbable run to the semifinals, where he faced "Our Tim," which was what the home fans called sixth-seeded Englishman Tim Henman. Ivanišević was trailing two sets to one when the match was interrupted by a lengthy rain delay. After it resumed, Ivanišević rallied to win the next two sets and the match. He advanced to play third-seeded Australian Patrick Rafter in the final, where Ivanišević battled the two-time major winner for five sets before prevailing 6–3, 3–6, 6–3, 2–6, 9–7. It was the only major win of Ivanišević's career.

2005 Wimbledon Women's Final

In 2001, the winner opposite Ivanišević on the women's side was American Venus Williams, claiming her second title in London. By 2005, however, fortunes had declined for Williams as battles with an abdominal injury and inconsistent play dropped her out of the top 10. She entered the 2005 Wimbledon tournament as the 14th seed.

Williams found her form at this Wimbledon, however, advancing to the final against top-seeded American Lindsay Davenport. Davenport won the first set 6-4, and the second went to a tiebreaker after Williams broke Davenport, who was serving for the match at 6-5. Williams won the tiebreaker and forced a deciding set. Serving at 4-5, Williams faced a match point down 30-40 but saved it and won the game. The set stretched into the 15th game, where Williams broke Davenport then held serve to win the title in the longest women's final in Wimbledon history.

GREATEST MOMENTS

The Greatest Match Ever Played

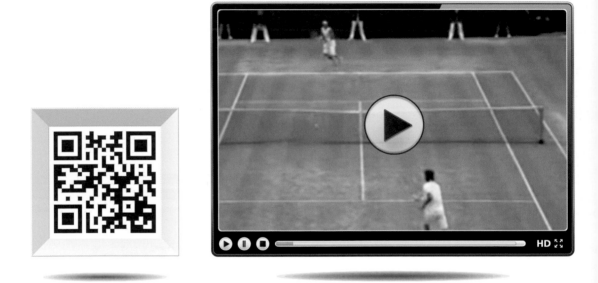

The longest men's final in Wimbledon history is widely considered to be the greatest tennis match played anywhere, ever. The 2008 final was a rematch of a colossal five-set battle in the 2007 final between Spain's Rafael Nadal and Swiss champion Roger Federer, who won his fifth straight Wimbledon title that year.

Entering Wimbledon, two-seed Nadal was coming off his fourth straight French Open, where he beat Federer. He picked up where he left off in Paris, winning the first two sets 6-4. But the then 12-time major winner had an answer. With neither man able to break serve, Federer won sets three and four in tiebreakers, with the fourth set taking 18 points. In the fifth set, Nadal finally broke Federer's serve again at 7-7, the first service break in 41 games. Nadal served out the match to win his first Wimbledon 6-4, 6-4, 6-7, 6-7, 9-7.

Clijster's Comeback

Only 35 days after ending a two-year sabbatical from the sport in 2009, Kim Clijsters was a U.S. Open champion again. The Belgian won the event in 2005 when she was just 22 years old. She spent 19 weeks as the top-ranked player in the world before she left the game in 2007 to start a family. Less than a month into her comeback at age 26, Clijsters was granted a wild card entry to the 2009 U.S. Open as a former champion.

Clijsters had a magical two weeks, becoming the first unseeded woman to win the tournament in the Open Era. She also became the first mother to win a Grand Slam event since Evonne Goolagong at Wimbledon in 1980. She beat four seeded players, including both Williams sisters, on her way to the final, where she won in straight sets and celebrated on the court with her 18-month-old daughter.

This early portrait of American women playing tennis is from the same year (1887) in which the first U.S. National Women's Singles Championship was held in Newport, RI.

Words to Understand:

derivative: something formed from something else, for example, a word

precursor: something that comes before something else and that often leads to or influences its development

prowess: great ability or skill

CHAPTER

THE ORIGINS OF TENNIS

No one can say with certainty where the word tennis comes from. It is commonly believed to be a **derivative** of the French word "tenez," a declaration meaning to hold, receive, or take—an instruction shouted from server to opponent.

BEFORE RACKETS

Prior to French involvement with the game, it traces back to ancient Egypt, where "tennis" may have come from a textile center located in Tinnis that used to make cloth for ball covers.

In 12th-century France, an early form of the game was "jeu de paume," which translates to game of the palm, played by hitting a sheepskin ball back and forth with the bare hand. The game was very popular with French royalty, like King Louis X, who commissioned the first indoor court. Soon, indoor courts were being constructed at royal palaces across Europe. Over the centuries, gloves were worn over bare hands, and then rackets were introduced in the 17th century. This was still an indoor game, however, the **precursor** to modern handball or squash, as the walls were in play.

LAWN TENNIS

The first modern tennis club is credited to Englishman Harry Gem, a military veteran and lawyer who, alongside his Spanish friend Augurio Perera, developed tennis as a game played outdoors on a croquet pitch in 1872.

In 1873, a British army major named Walter Wingfield patented a similar game that included a net with poles, balls, and rackets. The net was 7 feet high (2.1 m), and the courts were wider at the ends than they were in the center, but it is widely credited as the first version of the modern game.

DEFINING RULES

The distinguishing element of Wingfield's patent was his set of rules, which were published in the British newspaper The Field in March of 1874 in an article titled "The Major's Game of Lawn Tennis." Publicity was one aspect of Wingfield's marketing **prowess** as he began to produce boxed tennis sets and shipped them around the world.

With lawn mowers now widely in use, court construction and maintenance was simple, and the game spread in popularity under Wingfield's rules. The game could be played by single players or teams of two (on a wider court). Players received a score of 15 for each of the first three points (later reduced to 10 for the third point) and won the game on the fourth point. At 40-40, a margin of two points was required to win. A margin of two games was also the standard for winning a set, which went to the first player to reach six games. The first player to win two sets won the match. These rules remain unchanged today.

A Sphairistikè lawn tennis court as designed by Major Wingfield in 1874. The hourglass shape was retained in the 1875 MCC rules but replaced by a rectangular court in the AELTC rules, which governed the first Wimbledon Championship.

THE ALL ENGLAND CLUB

By 1875, the game had gained widespread popularity and was officially added to the activities at the All England Croquet Club, located in the town of Wimbledon, just outside London. The club adapted the game to suit its needs, creating the rectangular 78x27 foot (23.8x8.2 m) court with 26-foot (7.9 m) service lines. The net was lowered to 3 feet

The All England Lawn Tennis and Croquet Club has hosted the Championships at Wimbledon for both men and women since 1884.

(1 m) at the center. Service lines were also adjusted to 21 feet (6.4 m) from the net.

In July of 1877, the club hosted its first championship match between Spencer Gore and William Marshall in front of a crowd that paid the equivalent of 25 cents each to watch. Today, the location is famously known simply as Wimbledon but officially is the All England Lawn Tennis and Croquet Club, which continues to host the championship each July. The ladies' championship was added in 1884.

TENNIS IN AMERICA

American socialite Mary Outerbridge had sailed to Bermuda on holiday in January of 1874. While there, she witnessed British soldiers playing a game she had never seen before, hitting a ball back and forth with wooden rackets across a net. She talked to an officer, who helped her get one of Wingfield's sets, and returned to New York to show her brother her discovery.

Mary Outerbridge

Emilius Outerbridge was a member of the Staten Island Cricket and Baseball Club, in New York, where he set up the first tennis court in America. Later that year near Boston, Massachusetts, James Dwight set up a court with a set he had obtained from England. The first U.S. tournament was held on Dwight's court in 1876, and the first national championship was played on the Staten Island court in 1880.

RULES UNIFICATION

The game played in Boston was not identical to that played in Staten Island. The primary difference was the size of the ball being used. Although Dwight's tournament had adopted the All England Club rules, he used a larger ball. This discrepancy eventually led to the formation of the U.S. National Lawn Tennis Association in 1881, which unified the game's rules and regulations. Dwight served as president for 21 years.

The association sponsored the U.S. National Men's Single Championship in 1881 at Newport, Rhode Island. Won by 19-year-old Dick Sears, that was the precursor to today's U.S. Open tournament. The Women's Championship was added in 1887.

 **Text-Dependent Questions:**

1. Who commissioned the first indoor court in France?

2. In what year did the All England Croquet Club host its first championship match between Spencer Gore and William Marshall in front of a crowd that paid the equivalent of 25 cents each to watch?

3. The first U.S. tournament was held on James Dwight's court in what year?

Research Project:

Go online, and find images of old tennis balls, rackets, and various playing surfaces. Compare them to the equipment and courts of today. Examine how these items have improved over time and how each has changed the game of tennis.

American tennis player Maurice McLoughlin in the 1913 Challenge Round match against Anthony Wilding

Words to Understand:

petticoats: a skirt a woman or girl wears under a dress or outer skirt

decorum: correct or proper behavior that shows respect and good manners

burgeoning: growing or developing quickly

CHAPTER

FROM A GAME TO A SPORT

Tennis became the competitive sport we know it as today at the turn of the 20th century. In 1900, for example, Harvard graduate Dwight Davis commissioned a $750 silver bowl as the trophy for an international team tennis competition. The first Davis Cup was held in Boston between the United States and Great Britain and is still competed for to this day by more than 100 countries each year.

A SPORT FOR THE MASSES

The more inclusive a sport is, the more competitive it becomes. As tennis grew in popularity and moved out of country clubs and into public parks, the sport gained more exposure and attracted better athletes.

Maurice McLoughlin was the perfect example. The "California Comet" honed his lethal serve on public courts in his home state and used it to win the U.S. Championship in 1912. He took his serve-and-volley style of play to Wimbledon, the sport's other significant tournament, in 1913, but lost to the three-time defending champion Tony Wilding of New Zealand.

Team photo of seven women in sports dress
holding tennis rackets in the early 1900s

INTERNATIONAL ORGANIZATION

In 1913, the U.S. National tournament moved to Queens, New York, with the sport trying to organize on a global scale. The International Lawn Tennis Federation (ILTF) was formed and included clubs and federations from around the world.

The United States did not immediately recognize the ILTF as the sport's governing body, not joining the organization until after World War I.

SUZANNE LENGLEN

Frenchwoman Suzanne Lenglen is one of the best players in the history of the game. When she arrived at Wimbledon in 1919, however, she made headlines for more than just her game.

Traditionally, women in England played in corsets covered in blouses and layers of **petticoats**. Lenglen created a stir when she took the court wearing a one-piece dress that left her lower legs and forearms uncovered. Some female spectators left in disgust, missing a dazzling display of skill from Lenglen as the 20-year-old won the match and went on to win the title.

French tennis player Suzanne Lenglen at the French Championships 1920

CHANGING THE GAME

Lenglen was the primary force in turning the woman's game into a sport. As tennis writer Al Laney wrote, Lenglen "broke down barriers . . . substituting acrobatics and something of the art of the ballet where **decorum** had been the rule." Lenglen was an athlete, and playing the sport like one brought her a lot of attention.

Her popularity was on full display when she traveled to the United States for the first time to play the U.S. National Championship tournament. For her second-round match, 8,000 fans turned out to watch, which was the largest ever for a women's match in the United States. The fans were not amused when Lenglen was forced to retire due to illness. She made up for it at the 1922 Wimbledon tournament, where she dominated, winning the final match 6-2 6-0.

PROFESSIONAL TENNIS

By the 1920s, there was a **burgeoning** circuit of professional players who traveled from site to site playing tournaments for pay. These players, however, were banned by the ILTF from competing in events it oversaw, like the Davis Cup and Wimbledon. Lenglen turned pro in 1926 and had a successful career on that circuit.

In 1927, the professionals organized their own championship tournament, played in New York. Vinnie Richards was the winner of the first two U.S. Pro Championship tournaments.

HELEN WILLS MOODY

After Lenglen left for the pro circuit, Helen Wills Moody became the dominant player in the women's game. She won both the U.S. National Championship and Wimbledon in back-to-back years, 1927 and 1928. In fact, she was so dominant that she did not lose a single set from 1927 to 1932.

By 1933, she had not lost since being beaten by Lenglen in 1926. Moody was in the final of the U.S. National Championship against Helen Jacobs when she retired due to a back injury while trailing in the second set. She finished her career with eight Wimbledon and seven U.S. National titles.

Helen Wills Moody 1932

Bill Tilden

BILL TILDEN

Over on the men's side, the sport's dominant force was "Big Bill" Tilden. Tilden had the perfect mix of skill and showmanship that captivated fans. Although just 6'2" (1.9 m), Tilden was tall for a player of that era. His long legs gave him the ability to cover the court and get to most balls. He also had a powerful serve, a combination that won him both the U.S. National and Wimbledon titles in 1920. Tilden won six straight U.S. National titles from 1920 to 1925.

In one stretch in 1925, Tilden won 57 straight games. He continued to play as an amateur until 1931, when he turned pro. He became the main attraction on the pro tour, along with Englishman Fred Perry (who joined in 1936), a three-time Wimbledon and U.S. National Championship winner.

DON BUDGE

Oakland, California's, Don Budge took over as the best player in the men's game after Tilden and Perry turned pro. Budge won the first Grand Slam in tennis, capturing the Australian, French, U.S., and Wimbledon Championships in 1938.

Don Budge at the White City Stadium in Sydney, Australia

Text-Dependent Questions:

1. The first Davis Cup was held in Boston between which two countries?

2. Which French female athlete is one of the best tennis players in the history of the game?

3. Bill Tilden won how many straight games in one stretch in 1925?

Research Project:

Go to your local library, and check out a biography on one of the players from this chapter. Learn more about his or her tennis career, personal life, and accomplishments both on and off the court. Next, research a current player, and compare and contrast the kinds of challenges each faced in his or her own time.

Participants in a tennis party to aid Red Cross funds

 Words to Understand:

persevered: continued doing something or trying to do something even though it was difficult

circuit: a series of performances or sports events that are held or done in many different places

CHAPTER

THE OPEN ERA

Don Budge turned pro in the 1940s, continuing the trend of most of the top players. Once success in the amateur ranks was achieved, they left for the professional circuit. After World War II, players such as Frank Parker, Jack Kramer, and Pancho Gonzales all turned pro.

Through the 1940s and 1950s, professional tennis struggled to find a foothold with the sport's fans. The amateur events continued to be the ones that people cared about, and those events were controlled by the ILTF, which continued to bar pro players. The pro game **persevered**, however, with a men's tour organized by Kramer through the 1950s and into the 1960s.

Tennis grew as a recreational sport through the mid-20th century, with several clubs attracting dozens of members of both sexes, like this one in Gainsborough, UK.

ALTHEA GIBSON

The 1950s was a notable time in tennis for something more than just the growth of the professional game. In 1950, organizers of the U.S. National Women's Championship invited 23-year-old Althea Gibson to play in their tournament. Five-time major champion Alice Marble had lobbied fiercely for Gibson's inclusion. Gibson, a Harlem, New York, native, had captured Marble's attention with her superb showing on the American Tennis Association Tour (ATA). The ATA was a tour for blacks, who were formally barred from playing in United States Lawn Tennis Association (USLTA) tournaments.

Althea Gibson

Gibson had won four straight ATA women's titles when she was invited to play in the U.S. Nationals. She lost in the second round, but her accomplishment was massive. No black player had ever played on the courts at Forest Hills. Wrote New York *Daily Worker* sports editor Lester Rodney, "It is even a tougher personal Jim Crow-busting assignment than was Jackie Robinson's when he first stepped out of the Brooklyn Dodgers dugout." In 1959, Bob Ryland became the first black player in the men's game.

THE GAME OPENS UP

The professional game struggled along into the 1960s until Texas oil millionaire and founder of the American Football League, Lamar Hunt, decided to branch into tennis. In 1967, he founded World Championship Tennis, a professional tour that made an immediate splash by signing the top eight men's players, including John Newcombe and Cliff Drysdale. Hunt's aggression with signing players got the attention of Herman David, president of the All England Club, and in 1968 he announced that Wimbledon would allow professionals to compete. Rod Laver won the first "open" Wimbledon in August 1968, besting a field that featured 13 former champions. The success of the event prompted the organizers of the other majors to open their tournaments.

The ILTF and its members still refused to recognize professional players, however, so those who wanted to play in ILTF events like the Davis Cup still had to maintain amateur status. Arthur Ashe won the 1968 U.S. Open as an amateur, receiving no prize money.

Tony Roche won the first ever World Championship Tennis tournament, in January 1968 in Sydney, Australia.

Dennis Ralston was one of the original eight players in the 1968 World Championship Tennis tournament.

South African Cliff Drysdale was one of the "Handsome Eight" in the first World Championship Tennis tournament in 1968.

In 1970, former player Jack Kramer introduced another concept to the pro game with Grand Prix tennis. Players competed in designated tournaments and received points, which accumulated through the season. The top point earner won $25,000 in 1970. The system still exists as part of today's game as the Association of Tennis Professionals (ATP) World Tour Masters 1000 series, with points going toward each player's overall world ranking.

The classic scoreboard at the All England Club at Wimbledon

NEW RULES

For 100 years, the standard for winning a set had been the first player to win six games, provided the margin was at least two games. This rule sometimes resulted in very long matches. The most extreme example occurred in the first round of the men's 1969 Wimbledon tournament. Pancho Gonzales outlasted Charlie Pasarell 22–24, 1–6, 16–14, 6–3, 11–9 in a match that took more than five hours over two days to complete.

In 1971, the ILTF and other tennis organizations agreed on a rule change designed to reduce the duration of sets and matches. When the score in a set reached 8-8, the players competed in a tiebreaker, each serving two points and alternating until one player had reached seven points with a margin of at least two. In 1979, the rule changed to have the tiebreaker begin after 12 games.

THE ATP

The ILTF could not agree to accept professional tennis, and in 1971, the organization banned pros from all its events beginning with the 1972 season. In response, the male players founded the Association of Tennis Professionals (ATP). Kramer was executive director, and Cliff Drysdale was named president. The ILTF did not hold out for long after that, and in March 1972, the ATP and ILTF agreed to promote a unified **circuit** that allowed professional players at all events.

The first major action from the new ATP came in 1973, when Yugoslavian Nikki Pilic was suspended by the ILTF after he skipped the Davis Cup, meaning he could not play at Wimbledon. In a bold move, all the ATP players boycotted the tournament, and the power forever shifted to them.

Text-Dependent Questions:

1. Who was the first black player to play on the courts at Forest Hills?

2. In 1967, who founded World Championship Tennis?

3. In 1971, the ILTF and other tennis organizations agreed on a rule change designed to reduce the duration of sets and matches. Explain the change.

Research Project:

In this chapter we learned that Althea Gibson was the first black woman to play in the U.S. National Women's Championship in 1950. New York Daily Worker sports editor Lester Rodney wrote: "It is even a tougher personal Jim Crow-busting assignment than was Jackie Robinson's when he first stepped out of the Brooklyn Dodgers dugout." Get a group of friends together, and pick your favorite five sports. Divide up the work, and take a closer look at the first African American athletes who broke the color barrier to play in their respective sports. Share your research and thoughts with each other.

In 1970 Margaret Court won all four Grand Slam singles tournaments.

Words to Understand:

disparity: containing or made up of fundamentally different and often incongruous elements

crown jewel: the most valuable or attractive thing in a collection or group

bevy: a large group of people or things

CHAPTER

THE GAME PROGRESSES

In the 1970 season, Margaret Court achieved the Grand Slam, winning all four major events. The only thing that wasn't major was her paycheck. Court's winnings for capturing the sport's top tournaments were just $15,000. This was reflective of the **disparity** between the men's and women's tours. Women were routinely paid about 40 percent of what men made for the same tournaments. The most glaring example was perhaps the 1970 edition of the Jack Kramer-promoted Pacific Southwest Open in Los Angeles, where the men's champion received $12,500 compared to just $1,500 for the women's winner. In fact, only the top eight finishers for the women would win any money at all for competing.

A NEW TOUR

World Tennis magazine founder Gladys Heldman decided to help protest this inequality by putting up $5,000 to stage a competing tournament in Houston, Texas. She recruited the Virginia Slims cigarette brand as a sponsor, and they kicked in another $2,500. On September 23, 1970, nine women signed player contracts to start their own tour, sponsored by Virginia Slims, including five-time major winner Billie Jean King. This date is celebrated as the birthday of women's pro tennis.

The USLTA suspended the memberships of all women who joined the Virginia Slims Tour, barring them from competing in major events. The tour only grew, however, playing 19 tournaments in 1971 and adding sponsors such as the Ford Motor Company and Kmart. That season, King became the first woman to win more than $100,000 in prize money, including the $10,000 first prize at the one-year anniversary of the Houston event.

EQUALITY ACHIEVED

By 1972, the Virginia Slims Tour boasted 60 players, and its events totaled $600,000 in prize money. The **crown jewel** of the season was the Tour Championships tournament, with a $100,000 top prize. Meanwhile, the USLTA suffered through hosting major events featuring mostly minor players.

Evonne Goolagong won the most tour titles (12) on the 1972 Virginia Slims Tour.

Desperate to lure back all of the top players, the USLTA launched a rival tour in 1973 and signed stars such as Chris Evert and Evonne Goolagong. The association's tour could not match the prize money offered on the Virginia Slims circuit, however, which in 1973 had climbed to $775,000 and 22 events. The women formed their own association in July, called the Women's Tennis Association (WTA), with King as president. At the U.S. Open, the men and women competed for an equal total purse, and Court won the $25,000 first prize. John Newcombe of Australia won the men's title. At the end of that 1973 season, the Virginia Slims merged with the USLTA tour. The Slims tournaments were incorporated into the USLTA schedule, and all tournaments had a minimum $50,000 purse. The WTA, however, had effectively become the sport's governing body. Separating from the USLTA was the first of several progressive milestones for the WTA.

IN THE MONEY

With its **bevy** of talented and marketable stars like Evert, Goolagong, Hana Mandlikova, and Tracy Austin, the WTA Tour thrived. In 1976, Evert became the first player, and the first woman in any sport, to hit the $1 million mark in career earnings. In 1982, Martina Navratilova won $1 million in a single year. She won $2 million in prize money just two years later in 1984. In little more than a decade, the top earner on the women's tour went from $100,000 to $2 million. The rivalry between Evert and Navratilova was a large driver of the interest in the women's game. Mandlikova won her second major at the 1981 French Open and her

Chris Evert and Martina Navratilova are retired professional tennis players who engaged in an iconic rivalry for dominance in women's tennis in the 1970s and 1980s.

Chris Evert

Martina Navratilova

USTA
NATIONAL
TENNIS CENTER

August 29 –
September 11, 1988

US
OPEN

third major at the 1985 U.S. Open. Of the 17 majors played in between, either Evert or Navratilova won 16 of them. The women's game built on the foundation of this rivalry and never looked back. In 2014, American superstar Serena Williams earned more than $12 million.

On the men's side, the ATP was equally as successful. Stars like American Jimmy Connors and Swede Björn Borg became international household names in the 1970s and were joined on the tour in the 1980s by the likes of John McEnroe, Mats Wilander, Ivan Lendl, Stefan Edberg, and Boris Becker. When Borg retired at age 26 in 1983, he had earned a then-record $3.6 million in career prize money.

PARKING LOT PRESSER

By the mid-1980s, despite the upturn in financial fortunes for players, issues involving player fatigue to the marketing of the sport were causing the majority of the men to be unhappy with the direction of tennis. The ATP had their own organization,but the International Tennis Federation and the Men's International Professional Tennis Council ran the tour the players competed on. Players increasingly felt that things needed to change, so they could have more control over the system in which they were the star attraction.

The tipping point came at the U.S. Open in 1988. With the support of 16 of the top 20 ranked men, ATP CEO Hamilton Jordan, surrounded by other ATP officials and players including Wilander, held a press conference in the parking lot outside the stadium as tournament officials denied him a room in the facility. Jordan announced that beginning with the 1990 season, the players would form their own tour, one that focused on a fewer number of top-level tournaments mandatory for the top-ranked players, a successful system that exists to the present day.

THE MODERN GAME

Since the 1970s, the game has been very good to the players. Graphite and fiberglass rackets were introduced in 1976, increasing racket speed and shot power. By 1987, the last wooden rackets on tour were gone. Today's players grew up playing with lightweight composite rackets on both natural and synthetic courts, developing the skills that make the top players international superstars.

Tennis racket owned and used by President Gerald R. Ford at the White House. Ford played tennis at the tennis court on the grounds of the White House for exercise and stress relief.

Modern tennis rackets are made with synthetic composites like graphite frames and polyester strings.

Text-Dependent Questions:

1. In 1970, women were routinely paid about what percentage of what men made for the same tournaments?

2. In what year at the U.S. Open did the men and women compete for an equal total purse for the first time?

3. What types of rackets were introduced in 1976, increasing racket speed and shot power?

Research Project:

This chapter discusses the growth of the purse in tennis tournaments over the years for both female and male players. Fast-forward to today. Make a chart to show the purses awarded to the winners of the top major tournaments of the most recent season. How do these winnings compare to those of the early 1970s, when equality was first reached as men and women began competing for an equal total purse?

Roger Federer

Words to Understand:

emulating: trying to be like someone or something you admire

compatriots: a person from the same country as someone else

eclipsed: loss of power, success, or popularity due to someone or something else doing better

CHAPTER

MODERN-DAY STARS

The international appeal of tennis is reflected in the diverse makeup of the sport's top stars. From Argentina to Australia, champions from Juan Martin del Potro to Samantha Stosur have risen to the highest levels of the game, **emulating** the success of **compatriots** like Emerson, Hewitt, Sabatini, and Vilas. American stars have had their moments of great success as well and continue to do so as a new generation of players begins to emerge.

As the game has evolved entering this century, however, it is Europe that has produced the talent that dominates the slots at the top of the rankings and the major tournaments.

MEN

The top player in the men's game to start the 21st century is considered by most to bethe best to ever play the game. Swiss legend Roger Federer has done it all in tennis since he broke through to win his first tournament on the ATP Tour at Milan, Italy, in 2001. He has won more than 85 tournaments, third best of all time. This includes a record 17 major tournaments, with a record seven wins at Wimbledon.

Federer is one of history's most versatile players, excelling on every surface. Federer, Rafael Nadal, and Andre Agassi are the only men to achieve the career Grand Slam in the Open Era. Federer was the number one-ranked player in the world longer than any other man in the history of the rankings.

Rafael Nadal

Federer's closest rival on tour is 14-time major winner Rafael Nadal. At the beginning of his career, Nadal was known as a clay court specialist, like many Spaniards. The reputation was well earned as he has won about 70 percent of his career titles on clay. This includes a record nine French Open titles. His career record at Roland Garros was 70-2 after losing the 2015 quarterfinal.

From 2005 through 2007, he was undefeated on clay, winning 81 in a row. A career Grand Slam winner, Nadal became a threat to win on any surface. In 2008, he captured the difficult "Channel Slam," the name for winning both the French Open and Wimbledon in the same year, one of only four men to pull off the feat.

The third player to also win double-digit majors alongside Federer and Nadal is Serbia's Novak Djokovic. The Serb was late to the party when he joined the tour, as by the time he broke through with his first major win in 2008, Federer already had a dozen majors, and Nadal had three. Between 2008 and 2015 however, Djokovic won 10 majors, Nadal 11, and Federer 5.

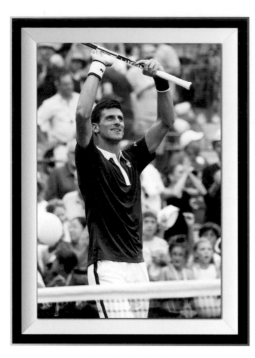

Novak Djokovic

Djokovic, six years younger than Federer and a year younger than Nadal, eventually **eclipsed** both in the rankings in 2011 after winning his third major at Wimbledon. Djokovic has been ranked number one longer than any other man except for Federer, Pete Sampras, Ivan Lendl, and Jimmy Connors. His 11 major titles are fifth most of all time.

Scotsman Andy Murray is known as the other member of the group called the "Big Four," along with Federer, Nadal, and Djokovic. These four dominated men's tennis beginning in 2005 with Nadal and Federer. Djokovic and Murray, who are the same age, joined the rivalry in 2008, when all four men were semifinalists at the U.S. Open. But of the four, Murray is a distant fourth. In his career record against the other three, Murray had lost about two-thirds of his matches, posting a losing record against all three.

Andy Murray

Murray has had relative success, however, being next best to the three superstars. He has two major titles, the 2012 U.S. Open, and most famously, the 2013 Wimbledon title, becoming the first Brit to win Wimbledon in 77 years.

Novak Djokovic of Serbia and Rafael Nadal of Spain pose with
trophies after the final match of the 2013 U.S. Open in New York City.

Grand Slam champion Marin Čilić of Croatia in action during his quarterfinal match at US Open 2015 at National Tennis Center in New York

Stanislas Wawrinka

Like England's Murray, Switzerland's other top player, Stanislas Wawrinka, also has two major titles. His first major came at the Australian Open in 2014, where he beat Nadal in four sets. In 2015, he captured the French Open title, denying Djokovic in his bid for the career Grand Slam with another four-set win.

Wawrinka found his form late in his career, not becoming a top 10 player until he was 28. He gives much of the credit for his career turnaround to coach Magnus Norman, a former second-ranked player from Sweden whom he hired in 2013. Seven-time major winner Mats Wilander called Norman "the best coach in the world," and Wawrinka's results are a testament to that. Wawrinka has 10 career titles.

By 2016, besides Wawrinka, Marin Čilić of Croatia was the only man outside the Big Four to win a major since 2009. Čilić won the 2014 U.S. Open, knocking off Federer in the semifinals. It was the 12th career win for Čilić, who won his 13th title the following month in Moscow.

The most successful season of Čilić's career came in 2014 under the influence of new coach Goran Ivanišević, a fellow Croatian and former Wimbledon champion. The two began working together in late 2013, and Čilić had newfound success, rising as high as eighth in the rankings. At 6'6" (2 m) with a dominant 130 mile-per-hour (209.2 km/h) serve, Čilić plays a game well suited to hard courts, the surface on which he has won all but two of his titles.

Marin Čilić

Grand Slam champion Serena Williams of the United States and Maria Sharapova of Russia after a quarterfinal match at Australian Open 2016 at Rod Laver Arena

Serena Williams

Maria Sharapova

WOMEN

Serena Williams has had a remarkable career. She turned 34 in 2015, and 20 years into her tennis journey, she was still the most dominant woman on the courts. She first reached number one in the world in 2002. Thirteen years later, Williams remained on top. The ride has not been a smooth one for Williams. In 2003 knee surgery derailed her season after she won her sixth major at Wimbledon.

Williams fought her way back to the top of the rankings by the end of 2008, but after winning her fourth Wimbledon in 2010, she stepped on a piece of glass in a restaurant, which ended her season. Never a quitter, she rehabbed and came back better than ever, winning eight more majors (21 total) and regaining the number one ranking.

Williams has been the greatest obstacle preventing the great career of Maria Sharapova from being even greater. The towering 6'2" (1.9 m) Russian has struggled to beat Williams, losing to her at six majors. At the 2004 Wimbledon Championship, however, a 17-year-old Sharapova made the final as a 13 seed, where she beat the top-seeded Williams in her first major final to shock the sport.

Since then, Sharapova has been ranked number one five times and has won the other three majors as well to complete the career Grand Slam. Sharapova is also one of the most popular athletes in the sport and, in fact, in all of sports. Mostly from endorsements, she earned more money ($30 million) than any female athlete in the world every year from 2005 through 2015.

Williams was second in worldwide female athlete earnings in 2015, and Denmark's Caroline Wozniacki was third. Wozniacki debuted on the WTA Tour just after her 15th birthday in 2005 and won her first title in 2008 in Sweden. She has collected more than 20 titles, which is in the top 25 all time. She has never, however, won a major.

Despite being ranked number one in the world for all but one week from October 2010 to January 2012, Grand Slam glory eluded Wozniacki. She lost the U.S. Open final twice, in 2009 to Kim Clijsters and to Williams in 2014. Wozniacki has a reputation for being one of the fittest women on the tour. In 2014 she ran in and completed the New York City marathon.

The Czech Republic's Petra Kvitová has the opposite problem to Wozniacki. One of the top players on the WTA Tour for years, she has never been able to claim the number one ranking. She has, however, been able to claim a major tournament title.

Kvitová had her first chance at major glory during the 2010 season, when she made it to the semifinal round at Wimbledon. Her stellar play continued into 2011, when she made the quarterfinals at the Australian Open before going on to win Wimbledon in straight sets over Sharapova. Soon after, she rose to number two in the rankings. Kvitová made two more major semifinals in 2012. In 2014 she won Wimbledon a second time, beating Victoria Azarenka.

Caroline Wozniacki

Petra Kvitová

Azarenka has played in four Grand Slam finals. This occurred in 2012 and 2013, when she made back-to-back finals in both the Australian and U.S. Opens. She posted identical results each year, winning the Australian Open, and losing the U.S. Open. At the Australian she beat Sharapova and Li Na, while in New York she lost both finals to Williams.

Those 2012 and 2013 seasons found Vika, as Azarenka is called by fellow players, at the top of her game. She claimed the number one ranking after her Australian Open win in 2012 and held it for 51 weeks through February of 2013, when Williams reclaimed it. Azarenka, who was born and raised in Belarus, has 17 career WTA singles titles.

Like Azarenka, Serbia's Ana Ivanovic is a former number one-ranked player and major tournament winner. Ivanovic won her first WTA title at age 17 in Canberra, Australia. Continued strong play saw her make the quarterfinal round on the clay at Roland Garros, her best surface. In 2007 she made her first Grand Slam final, also at the French Open, which she lost to Justine Henin.

In 2008 Ivanovic made her second major final at the Australian Open, losing to Sharapova. Her breakthrough came when she returned to the French Open that year and made the final again. This time, she won, defeating Dinara Safina. For 12 weeks between the French Open and the U.S. Open in 2008, Ivanovic was ranked number one in the world. In 2015 she entered the year ranked number five and made her fifth major semifinal, again at the French Open.

Victoria Azarenka

Ana Ivanovic

Caroline Wozniacki of Denmark in action during a US Open 2015 first round match at Arthur Ashe stadium in New York

Text-Dependent Questions:

1. Who was the number one-ranked player in the world longer than any other man in the history of the rankings?

2. Who are the members of the group called the "Big Four"?

3. Which female player earned more money ($30 million) than any female athlete in the world every year from 2005 through 2015?

Research Project:

Pick your favorite female and male tennis players, and visit their Web sites and social media accounts to get a closer look inside their lives. Do they act as role models for today's youth? Do they give back to the community? What are they doing to mentor young athletes? Which charities do they support? After learning more about these actions, do you feel any differently about them? Write each athlete a letter to share your support or suggestions for improvement in these areas, and send it.

JUSTINE HENIN

BJÖRN BORG

MARTINA NAVRATILOVA

ANDRE AGASSI AND STEFFI GRAF

SERENA WILLIAMS

ROD LAVER

RAFAEL NADAL

PETE SAMPRAS

VENUS WILLIAMS

ROGER FEDERER

INTERNATIONAL TENNIS HALL OF FAME

MARGARET COURT

The International Tennis Hall of Fame is located in Newport, Rhode Island. It was established in 1954 and has more than 200 player inductees. The hall and accompanying museum underwent a substantial renovation that was completed in 2015.

Scan here to go to the Tennis Hall of Fame website.

CHAPTER

THE GREATEST PLAYERS IN TENNIS

What would Rod Laver have done with a graphite racket and modern-day tennis shoes? This is the kind of question that frames the debate as to who is the best tennis player of all time. Comparing across eras is difficult to do.

Few would argue that Serena Williams would not easily have beaten Margaret Court given Wiliams's comparatively superior power and athleticism. Yet Court was the dominant player in the women's game at the start of the Open Era, winning eight of the era's first 12 majors. However, Williams versus Navratilova or Steffi Graf in their primes would be a match worth inventing time travel to see.

All we have is to examine what a player did in the time he or she played on a level field with other players of the same era. The fitness and nutrition regimens that today's players live by consist of elements that players from past eras did not consider. Diet, rest, and weight training are just a few examples of these elements considered crucial to today's players that were lightly regarded by those who starred in the 1980s and earlier.

Yet star they did, and the accomplishments and skills of players throughout the 20th century cannot be discounted when considering the game's greats. No matter the era, the physical skills of flexibility, balance, and hand-eye coordination are essential. As an individual sport, the mental aspects of the game are particularly important in tennis. Whether in 1960 or 2016, the elements of confidence, anticipation, perseverance, and a will to win are hallmarks of tennis champions.

While the physical and mental skills of the game's great players may be similar, champions can be remarkably different emotionally. Players like Boris Becker, Jimmy Connors, and John McEnroe wore their hearts on their sleeves and are far removed from the days of gentlemanly decorum that was expected on the court. Yet others are remarkably stoic, like Federer, Borg, and Stefan Edberg.

More than 100 years of competition have yielded great players from many eras, the ones who keep fans coming back year after year.

MEN

In the early years of his career, few would have predicted that Roger Federer would go on to become the greatest player in the game's history. However, in the minds of most experts, that is exactly what happened. With his slight build and long hair, Federer debuted on tour in 1998 but failed to win a tournament until 2001. After that, his brilliance quickly became evident.

Federer won his eighth tournament in 2003 at the Wimbledon Championships, his first major. He took over as the top-ranked player in the world after winning his second major at the Australian Open in 2004. He held the number one rank for a record 237 straight weeks.

Federer's nemesis at the apex of his career was Spain's Rafael Nadal. Nadal and Federer met more than 30 times in their careers, with Nadal winning about two-thirds of the matches. Nadal was especially good on clay, winning 13 of 15 against Federer. Clay was Nadal's best surface. He won the French Open, the clay court major, nine times in the 10 years from 2005 to 2014.

Nadal finally eclipsed Federer as the world's top-ranked player after winning the Olympic gold medal in August of 2008, snapping Federer's 237-week string. Nadal is fifth all time in career singles tournament victories. He completed the career Grand Slam when he won the U.S. Open in 2010.

The U.S. Open was the setting for the final match of American Pete Sampras in 2002. Sampras won the tournament in that last performance to claim his 14th major victory, a record that has since been passed only by Federer.

Sampras is sixth all time in career singles tournament wins. His main weapon was a dominating

Roger Federer

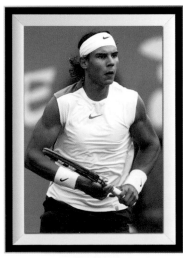

Rafael Nadal

Pete Sampras

serve delivered with power and accuracy. He is widely regarded as one of the sport's best servers, and many believe only Federer was better as an all-around player. He was, however, unable to win the French Open in his career. The fast grass courts of Wimbledon were where Sampras shone, winning six titles in seven years from 1993 to 2000.

Sampras grew up in California idolizing Australia's Rod Laver. The two met in 1982 when Sampras was 11, and the young prodigy got the chance to play his hero. At the time, Laver was five years retired from one of the sport's best careers. Laver twice achieved the Grand Slam, winning all four major tournaments in the same calendar year. He did so once as an amateur in 1962 and then again as a pro in 1969.

Before 1968, the start of the Open Era, pros were banned from competing in the major tournaments. Had Laver been allowed to compete during the five years he was banned, from 1963 to 1967, he might well be the record holder for career majors.

Sweden's Björn Borg never came close to a Grand Slam, either in a single year or in his career. He gave himself the chance only once in his career, when he played the Australian Open in 1974. Borg never played the tournament again, claiming it was inconveniently scheduled. He preferred to prepare for the French Open instead, which he won six times, including four in a row from 1978 to 1981.

Borg also won five straight Wimbledon titles from 1976 to 1980. Borg did lose four U.S. Open finals, but losing was rare for Borg at majors as he won a record 41 percent of those he played. He was the first player to earn $1 million in prize money. Borg retired at only age 26.

Rod Laver

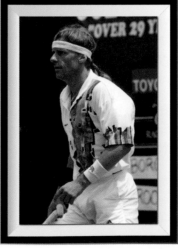

Björn Borg

Andre Agassi

Bill Tilden

Ivan Lendl

At age 26, Andre Agassi was just getting started. The brash American from Las Vegas, Nevada, had three majors under his belt when he turned 26 in 1996. At 29, he won the 1999 French Open to complete the career Grand Slam. He would win four more majors, including the 2003 Australian Open at age 32. Agassi was very good for a long time. He was ranked number one in the world six different times between 1995 and 2003.

Agassi could play on any surface, making the finals of each major tournament at least twice. He also won the 1996 Olympic gold medal. Agassi played from the baseline with accurate ground strokes and was one of the best returners of serve ever.

One of history's biggest serves belonged to "Big Bill" Tilden. The Philadelphia native was just 6'2" (1.9 m), but for the early 20th century, that was considered tall, especially for a tennis player. Tilden played his first U.S. National Championship tournament in 1916 at age 23, but it was in 1920 when his career began to flourish. That year, he won his first of back-to-back Wimbledon titles as well as the first of six straight U.S. National titles.

Tilden never played the Australian Open but did make two French Open finals. In his career, he won nearly 90 percent of his matches at major tournaments. Between 1924 and 1926, he won a record 95 consecutive matches.

Another player who used a power game to dominate opponents was Czechoslovakia's (now the Czech Republic) Ivan Lendl. Lendl knew how to win tournaments, and only one player has more career singles titles than he does.

Lendl was one of the most dominant players of the 1980s, when he made at least one Grand

John McEnroe

Jimmy Connors

Slam final every season from 1981 to 1989 and was ranked number one in the world eight times from 1983 to 1989, with one stretch lasting 157 weeks. Lendl was best on either clay or hard courts, winning multiple titles at the Australian, French, and U.S. Opens. He was never able to win at Wimbledon to complete the career Grand Slam, losing back-to-back finals there in 1986 and 1987.

American John McEnroe had the opposite problem to Lendl. The Queens, New York, native was dominant on the fast surfaces at Wimbledon and the U.S. Open, but the French clay was his nemesis. From 1980 to 1984, McEnroe was a Wimbledon finalist all five years, winning three. At Flushing Meadow, he won three straight U.S. Opens from 1979 to 1981.

McEnroe was ranked number one in the world on 14 separate occasions. Between July of 1983 and September of 1988, the number one ranking switched between McEnroe and Lendl 11 times. The two rivals played 36 times, with Lendl winning 21, including two of three Grand Slam finals. Famous for his petulant on-court outbursts, fans either loved him or hated him.

McEnroe's other main rival at the top of the men's game was fellow American Jimmy Connors. Connors grew up near St. Louis, Missouri, and was an All-American in tennis at the University of California, Los Angeles (UCLA). He was ranked top four in the world from 1973 to 1987, including five years ending the season at number one.

Unlike McEnroe, Connors was a fan favorite, especially later in his career. He has called his 1991 U.S. Open tournament "the best 11 days of my tennis career." In that tournament, the 39-year-old Connors electrified the crowds, making it all the way to the semifinals. He may have lost that tournament, but in his career, he won more tournaments than any player in the game's history.

WOMEN

They called her "Fräulein Forehand." Germany's Steffi Graf not only had a deadly forehand but was in perfect command of all the other strokes as well. Graf won her first title at 17 in April of 1986 then proceeded to win seven more tournaments that year. Graf won her first major at Wimbledon the next year and won at least one major every year after until 1997.

Graf's best year was 1988, when she won all four majors and the Olympic gold medal for what is known as the Golden Slam, an unmatched feat. Starting with the 1988 Australian Open, Graf won eight of the next nine majors. She spent more time as the number one-ranked player, including a record 186 weeks in a row, more than any woman ever has before or since.

Graf took over the position of number one in the world from Martina Navratilova in August of 1987. Navratilova had been number one for the preceding 90 straight weeks. She split 18 career meetings with Graf, losing four of six Grand Slam finals the two played. Navratilova won most of her Grand Slam finals in her career, however.

The native of the then Czechoslovakia was good on all surfaces, making 32 Grand Slam finals in her career and attaining the career Grand Slam by winning the U.S. Open in 1983. She was most comfortable, however, on the grass at Wimbledon, where she won nine times, including six in a row from 1982 to 1987.

Navratilova's main rival in her career was not Graf but rather Floridian Chris Evert. Evert and Navratilova dominated women's tennis from the mid-1970s to the mid-1980s. They played 80

Steffi Graf

Martina Navratilova

Chris Evert

matches, with Navratilova winning 47. Evert had the upper hand on clay however, winning 11 of their 14 matches. Evert was excellent on every surface, making a record 34 Grand Slam finals, but was especially good on clay. She won a record seven times at the French Open and won nearly 95 percent of her clay court matches in her career.

Only Navratilova has more career tournament wins than Evert. Evert has the best winning percentage of any player in the Open Era, at almost 90 percent.

Serena Williams has the fifth-best winning percentage in the history of the women's game. After learning to play the game growing up in Los Angeles, she turned pro in 1995 and won her first title in 1999. Her first major tournament win came at the U.S. Open that same year.

Williams has won each of Wimbledon, the Australian Open, and the U.S. Open six times, including winning Wimbledon and the Australian Open in 2015. She also won the French Open that year to give her one less than the Open Era record of 22. Given her dominance even at age 34, she will likely at least match the record in 2016.

Australian Margaret Court holds the record for most career majors at 24, although 13 of her wins came before the Open Era. Still, winning 11 majors in the Open Era is fifth best behind only Graf, Williams, Evert, and Navratilova. Court and Graf are the only two Open Era women to achieve the Grand Slam by winning all four majors in the same year. She did it in 1970, in the midst of winning eight of nine majors. Only a semifinal loss at Wimbledon in 1969 prevented her from winning nine in a row.

Serena Williams

Margaret Court

Billie Jean King *Monica Seles* *Venus Williams*

In 1970, Court won 21 tournaments, an Open Era record. In both 1969 and 1973 she won 18 titles. No other woman has won more than 17 in a season.

Billie Jean King is the player who won 17 tournaments, achieved in 1971. King grew up in California, learning to play on the public courts of Long Beach. King's 12 majors (nine in the Open Era) demonstrate her prowess on the court, but her other contributions to the sport are much heralded also.

King was cofounder of the rogue Virginia Slims tour and president of the WTA. One of her most famous exploits was the nationally televised Battle of the Sexes, a three set match against then 55-year-old former top-ranked men's pro Bobby Riggs in 1973. Twenty-nine at the time, King won all three sets, saying that if she didn't win the match, "It would ruin the women's tour."

King's eight Open Era major victories rank just behind the nine of Monica Seles. Born in the former Yugoslavia, Seles turned pro in February 1989 and promptly won her first tournament in May.

Seles shot to the top of the rankings in short order. Starting with the 1990 French Open, she won eight of the next 12 major tournaments (all except Wimbledon) and was ranked number one in the world for 113 weeks. She was just 19 years old. Her last major victory may have been her most impressive, however. It came at the 1996 Australian Open, nearly three full years after a fan stabbed Seles during a match in Germany. Seles showed remarkable fortitude in climbing back to the top.

Seles's skills were in decline by the time Venus Williams joined the tour full-time in 1997. The two played 10 times before Seles retired in 2003, with Williams winning nine. By 2003,

Justine Henin

Martina Hingis

Williams had two Wimbledon and two U.S. Open titles under her belt. She beat younger sister Serena to win the 2001 U.S. Open.

Beginning with the 2002 French Open, the sisters played in four straight Grand Slam finals. Serena won them all. Venus played best on the grass at Wimbledon, where she was a finalist eight times. She won five titles. Her three finals losses there were all to her sister. Venus has a 7-7 record in Grand Slam finals. Six of the losses were to Serena.

Venus had a much easier time with Belgium's Justine Henin than she did with Serena. Including a win in the 2001 Wimbledon final, Williams beat Henin seven out of nine times. Henin did much better against the rest of the women's field, however. From 2003 to 2007, she won seven majors and the 2004 Olympic gold medal.

Henin was ranked number one in the world on four separate occasions, including a 61-week stretch beginning in 2007. She is 12th all time on the list of career tournament wins, a very impressive ranking given that she quit the sport in 2008 at just age 25, while still ranked number one in the world.

Number one in the world is where Swiss star Martina Hingis was used to being ranked in the late 1990s. Named for her Czech mother's idol, Martina Navratilova, Hingis won the Lipton Championships in Miami in 1997 to knock Graf off the top of the rankings for the last time. Hingis held the top spot for 80 weeks. In that span, she made four straight Grand Slam finals, winning all but the French Open.

Hingis won the 12th most titles of any female player (tied with Henin) before retiring from singles play in 2007. She made a return to the game on the Grand Slam doubles circuit in 2013 at age 32. In 2015 Hingis won five major doubles or mixed doubles titles.

Career Snapshots

Men

BILL TILDEN 1916-1930

138 Career Singles Titles (amateur)
10 majors
Ranked world #1 1920-26

JIMMY CONNORS 1972-1996

109 Career Singles Titles
8 majors
268 weeks ranked world #1

ROD LAVER 1963-1976

52 Career Singles Titles
11 majors
Ranked world #1 1964-70

PETE SAMPRAS 1988-2002

64 Career Singles Titles
14 majors
286 weeks ranked world #1

JOHN MCENROE 1978-1992

77 Career Singles Titles
7 majors
170 weeks ranked world #1

ANDRE AGASSI 1986-2006

60 Career Singles Titles
8 majors
101 weeks ranked world #1

BJÖRN BORG 1973-1993

64 Career Singles Titles
11 majors
109 weeks ranked world #1

ROGER FEDERER 1998- Present

87 Career Singles Titles
17 majors
302 weeks ranked world #1

IVAN LENDL 1978-1994

94 Career Singles Titles
14 majors
270 weeks ranked world #1

RAFAEL NADAL 2001- Present

67 Career Singles Titles
14 majors
141 weeks ranked world #1

All the above athletes are members of the Hall of Fame
with the exception of current players.

Women

MARGARET COURT 1960-1975

79 Career Singles Titles
24 majors
Ranked world #1 for six years

MONICA SELES 1989-2007

53 Career Singles Titles
9 majors
178 weeks ranked world #1

BILLIE JEAN KING 1959-1983

67 Career Singles Titles
12 majors
Ranked world #1 for six years

JUSTINE HENIN 1999-2011

43 Career Singles Titles
7 majors
117 weeks ranked world #1

STEFFI GRAF 1982-1999

107 Career Singles Titles
22 majors
377 weeks ranked world #1

VENUS WILLIAMS 1994- Present

47 Career Singles Titles
7 majors
11 weeks ranked world #1

CHRIS EVERT 1982-1999

154 Career Singles Titles
18 majors
260 weeks ranked world #1

MARTINA HINGIS 1994- Present

43 Career Singles Titles
5 majors
209 weeks ranked world #1

MARTINA NAVRATILOVA 1975-2006

167 Career Singles Titles
18 majors
332 weeks ranked world #1

SERENA WILLIAMS 1995- Present

69 Career Singles Titles
21 majors
278 weeks ranked world #1

According to the Physical Activity Council, participation in tennis by kids age 6 to 17 rose 31 percent from 2000 to 2012.

Words to Understand:

novelty: the quality or state of being new, different, and interesting

protégé: a young person who is taught and helped by someone who has knowledge and experience

baseliner: a tennis player who stays on or near the baseline and seldom moves to the net

CHAPTER

THE FUTURE OF TENNIS

In the changing landscape of American sports, tennis officials and experts in the United States see an opportunity to grow their sport. Traditional American team sports like football, hockey, and soccer have come under intense scrutiny due to the increased awareness of the prevalence of concussions in those sports. As parents are discouraging their kids from participating in sports that carry the risk of violent collision, individual sports like tennis have benefitted. From 2000 to 2012, the Physical Activity Council reports that participation in tennis is up 31 percent among kids age 6 to 17.

BUILDING THE BASE

The challenge has become how to keep kids interested in the sport once they have been introduced to it. The Tennis Industry Association believes that the first impression is key to future participation. To heighten initial engagement upon introduction, the group has suggested the following:

- Loosening club membership rules

- Holding open houses at clubs and having "Bring a friend" days

- Introducing options for shorter matches, speed tennis or short course tennis

The idea is to make the sport more appealing to the next generation of potential players. Even at the collegiate level, there is concern about keeping tennis programs relevant. College tennis's governing body, the Intercollegiate Tennis Association, introduced changes in 2014 designed to speed up matches while making them more entertaining. The three biggest changes were these:

- Going to no-advantage scoring, meaning the requirement for players to win games by a two-point margin is removed

- Instead of playing a regular third set, immediately going to a tiebreaker when tied at one set all

- Limiting doubles matches to a single set

MAKE SOME NOISE

"Quiet, please." It's a familiar refrain from the umpire's chair for anyone who has attended or watched a tennis match. Traditionally, fans sit quietly during play on the court, cheering only

Fans at Rod Laver Arena watch a semifinal match between Andy Murray of the UK and David Ferrer of Spain in Melbourne, Australia.

when the point is won. It is an age-old standard that is being challenged in certain quarters.

In the National Collegiate Athletic Association (NCAA)'s Big 12 Conference for the 2015 season, heckling of players was not only permitted, but it was encouraged during play. To be fair, baseball players hit 95 mile-per-hour (152.9 km/h) fastballs, basketball players sink free throws, and football placekickers make field goals with fans in full throat. The behavior is a **novelty** in tennis, however, and allowing it is designed to engage fans by allowing them to do more than just watch.

The change actually was suggested by Texas Christian University coach David Roditi. With tennis programs being dropped at big division I schools like Arizona State, Maryland, and Kansas, he realized the importance of creating an atmosphere to attract new fans to the matches. The Big 12 agreed, and the future may see the "Roditi Rule" spread to other campuses in the country.

FAST4

At the pro level, there also has been experimentation of ways to speed matches up, including FAST4. In January 2015, Roger Federer and Lleyton Hewitt played a FAST4 match in Sydney, Australia. Under the FAST4 format, the following rules apply:

- Singles matches are played as the best of three shortened sets.

- Each set is the first to four games, with a short tiebreaker to be played at three-all.

- The tiebreaker is first to five points, with a sudden death point at four-all.

- There is no advantage scoring.

- There are no service lets.

- Changeovers are 60 seconds with no sitting for players.

- There are only 90 seconds between sets, but the players can sit.

The Australian match was just an exhibition, and it would be a strange future indeed if the format is ever adopted at the sport's highest level. Experts do predict, however, that FAST4 will become the trademark at many of the sport's lower levels as clubs and colleges seek to attract players and fans.

FUTURE STARS

EUGENIE BOUCHARD

The top-ranked Canadian female player experienced both success and adversity early in her career. In 2013 Bouchard was named WTA Newcomer of the Year after jumping up to number 32 in the rankings at just 19 years old. In 2014, she made two Grand Slam semifinals and was a finalist at a third, losing at Wimbledon. No woman won more Grand Slam matches that season than Bouchard, who was named WTA Most Improved Player for the year.

Eugenie Bouchard

NICK KYRGIOS

Like Bouchard, Australia's Nick Kyrgios burst onto the tour as a teen sensation. His impact been felt where it counts the most, and that is in the major tournaments. In 2014, at just 19 years old, Kyrgios announced himself by beating Rafael Nadal on Centre Court at Wimbledon, advancing all the way to the quarterfinals. He also made the quarters at the 2015 Australian Open and in his short career has beaten top 10 players Federer, Wawrinka, and Milos Raonic, along with Nadal.

Nick Kyrgios

BELINDA BENCIC

When Switzerland's Belinda Bencic made the quarterfinals at the U.S. Open in 2014 at age 17, she became the youngest to do so on the women's side since fellow Swiss Hingis did it in 1997. Bencic is the **protégé** of coach Melanie Molitor, who is Hingis's mother. In 2015 Bencic won her first two titles, at Eastbourne and at the Canadian Masters in Toronto, where she beat six top players.

TAYLOR TOWNSEND

Chicago, Illinois, native Taylor Townsend had a stellar junior career. In 2012 she became the first American to be ranked number one in juniors in 30 years. Her serve and volley game is a breath of fresh air in a **baseliners** era. She has been criticized for a poor serve, sloppy footwork, and a lack of fitness but can hit a variety of shots and covers the court with surprising quickness. None other than Serena Williams herself has called Townsend's game "the future of tennis."

Belinda Bencic

Taylor Townsend

All England Lawn Tennis and Croquet Club,
Wimbledon, London, England

Arthur Ashe Stadium,
Flushing, New York

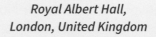

Stade Roland Garros,
Paris, France

Royal Albert Hall,
London, United Kingdom

Rod Laver Arena,
Melbourne, Australia

Aviva Centre,
Toronto, Canada

lob: a high return aimed above and beyond an opponent who is close to the net.

love: zero points in a game or set. It might come from the French for egg, l'oeuf.

match: a singles or doubles competition made up of a number of sets. Women's matches are two out of three sets, and men's are three of five.

match point: when a player could win the whole match if he or she wins the next point.

out: when a ball lands outside the court and does not touch a line.

passing shot: when a player returns the ball and it goes past an opponent who is rushing the net.

point: how the score is kept during games. A player wins points when the opponent missing the ball, hits the ball out of the court or into the net, or double faults.

serve: how each point starts. A player tosses the ball up and strikes it as hard as possible diagonally into the service box on the other side of the net.

set: how the score is kept in a match. The first player to seven games wins, but if both are tied at six games, the winner must win two more games than the opponent.

smash: a powerful, overhead shot most often used to return a high, soft shot.

topspin: when a player puts a top-to-bottom spin on the ball so that it dips toward the court after being hit. This way, the ball is more likely to stay low and remain in play.

underspin: when a player puts a bottom-to-top spin on the ball so that it loses speed and bounces softly, also called a slice.

unforced error: a bad shot a player makes that does not involve the opponent, either hitting the ball into the net or outside the lines.

volley: a shot made before the ball bounces in. This happens most often close to the net.

CHRONOLOGY

1877: In July, the All England Croquet Club, located in the London suburb of Wimbledon, hosts its first lawn tennis championship, the predecessor to Wimbledon.

1881: First men's U.S. Championship played at Newport Casino, Newport, R.I., predecessor to the U.S. Open, sponsored by the newly created U.S. National Lawn Tennis Association.

1905: First men's Australian Championship is played, predecessor to the Australian Open.

1913: International Lawn Tennis Federation is founded.

1919: Suzanne Lenglen wins her first Wimbledon title.

1925: First men's and women's French Championships is played, predecessor to the French Open.

1938: Twenty-three-year-old Don Budge becomes the first to win the four major championships Australia, France, Wimbledon, and the U.S. - a feat that becomes known as the Grand Slam.

1950: Jack Kramer creates the first professional tour.

1968: The "Open Era" of tennis begins with professionals allowed to enter tournaments.

1970: The tiebreaker is introduced.

1972: Male players form the Association of Tennis Professionals (ATP).

1973: Female players create their own Women's Tennis Association (WTA).

1976: Graphite and fiberglass rackets are introduced.

1987: Wood rackets are no longer used on the pro tennis tours.

1990: ATP Championship Series is introduced.

2010: John Isner and Nicholas Mahut play an 11 hour and five minute match at Wimbledon. Isner wins the final set 70-68.

2013: Scotsman Andy Murray wins Wimbledonn to become the first British man to win in nearly 80 years.

Tennis Today: Serbia's Novak Djokovic won his sixth Australian Open title in 2016, and in doing so set a new record for total ATP ranking points with 16,790. To put that achievement in perspective, Djokovic has been so dominant, winning 5 of the last 7 majors, including the 2016 Aussie, that he had nearly double the ATP rankings points than second ranked Andy Murray.

Twenty one times Grand Slam champion Serena Williams in action during her quarterfinal match against Venus Williams at US Open 2015 at National Tennis Center in New York

Rafael Nadal at the Australian Open, in Melbourne, Australia

FURTHER READING:

Malinowski, Scoop. *Facing Nadal: Symposium of a Champion.* New York, NY: Scoop Malinowski, 2015

Redban, Bill. *Roger Federer: The Inspirational Story of Tennis Superstar Roger Federer (Roger Federer Unauthorized Biography, Switzerland, Tennis Books).* Seattle, WA: CreateSpace Independent Publishing Platform, 2015

Parsons, John. *The Tennis Book*: London, England: Carlton Books, 2012

INTERNET RESOURCES:

Association of Tennis Professionals http://www.atpworldtour.com/en

Women's Tennis Association http://www.wtatennis.com/

United States Tennis Association https://www.usta.com/

International Tennis Hall of Fame https://www.tennisfame.com/

VIDEO CREDITS:

The Match of the Century (pg 8)   https://www.youtube.com/watch?v=P6xiG4_rAmQ

1980 Wimbledon Men's Final (pg 9)   https://www.youtube.com/watch?v=Yf0yfEfvMHE

1984 French Open Men's Final (pg 10)   https://www.youtube.com/watch?v=6S7RajqgN-A

Golden Slam (pg 11)   https://www.youtube.com/watch?v=fHUzPaxSM7M

The Fourth Time Is the Charm (pg 12)   https://www.youtube.com/watch?v=A_U6kVFe_JE

2005 Wimbledon Women's Final (pg 13)   https://www.youtube.com/watch?v=_iS_-J8r3nM

The Greatest Match Ever Played (pg 14)   https://www.youtube.com/watch?v=IfBX0IkcqLg

Clijster's Comeback (pg 15)   https://www.youtube.com/watch?v=oIkZp8-8NGI

QR CODES AND LINKS TO THIRD-PARTY CONTENT

You may gain access to certain third-party content ("Third-Party Sites") by scanning and using the QR Codes that appear in this publication (the "QR Codes"). We do not operate or control in any respect any information, products, or services on such Third-Party Sites linked to by us via the QR Codes included in this publication, and we assume no responsibility for any materials you may access using the QR Codes. Your use of the QR Codes may be subject to terms, limitations, or restrictions set forth in the applicable terms of use or otherwise established by the owners of the Third-Party Sites. Our linking to such Third-Party Sites via the QR Codes does not imply an endorsement or sponsorship of such Third-Party Sites, or the information, products, or services offered on or through the Third- Party Sites, nor does it imply an endorsement or sponsorship of this publication by the owners of such Third-Party Sites.

PICTURE CREDITS

INDEX